Contents

Meet the velociraptor

The velociraptor was small

but fast.

Adult velociraptors could run

64 kilometres (40 miles)

per hour in short bursts.

DINOSAURS

VELOCIRAPTOR

by Tammy Gagne

Raintree is an imprint of Capstone Global Library Limited, a company incorporated in England and Wales having its registered office at 264 Banbury Road, Oxford, OX2 7DY – Registered company number: 6695582

www.raintree.co.uk
myorders@raintree.co.uk

Edited by Hank Musolf
Designed by Charmaine Whitman
Picture research by Kelly Garvin
Production by Laura Manthe
Illustrated by Jon Hughes/Capstone Press
Originated by Capstone Global Library Ltd
Printed and bound in India

ISBN 978 1 4747 5220 6 (hardback)
22 21 20 19 18
10 9 8 7 6 5 4 3 2 1

ISBN 978 1 4747 5226 8 (paperback)
22 21 20 19 18
10 9 8 7 6 5 4 3 2 1

British Library Cataloguing in Publication Data
A full catalogue record for this book is available from the British Library.

Design elements: Shutterstock/Krasovski Dmitri

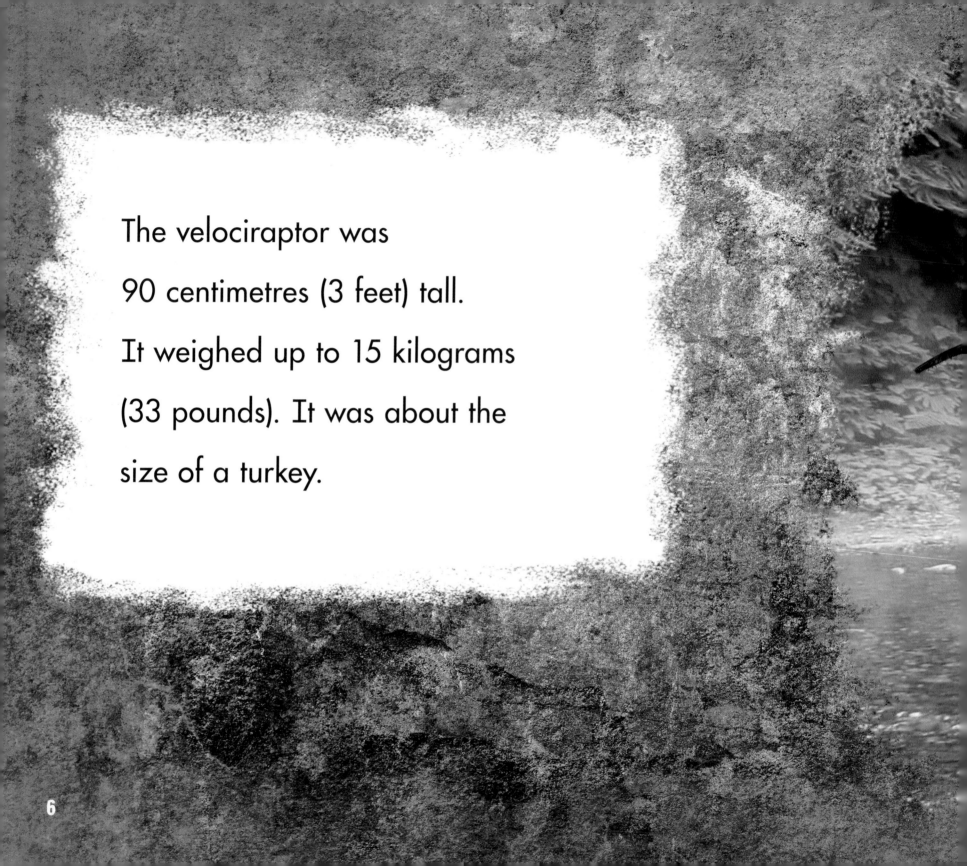

The velociraptor was
90 centimetres (3 feet) tall.
It weighed up to 15 kilograms
(33 pounds). It was about the
size of a turkey.

This dinosaur was bird-like. It had feathers on its short front legs. But the velociraptor could not fly.

The speedy thief

The name *velociraptor* means "speedy thief". The velociraptor was a carnivore. It had three claws on each front foot.

It had a large claw on each back foot. It used these claws for hunting its prey. The claws helped it to catch prey quickly.

Velociraptor fossils

The velociraptor lived about 70 million years ago. Velociraptor fossils have been found in Asia. Most were buried deep in the desert.

Dinosaur fossils have been found with velociraptor bite marks in them. The marks match the velociraptor's widely spaced teeth.

On the hunt

Scientists think this species hunted in packs. Velociraptor fossils have been found together with prey. The velociraptors could have been fighting over the food.

The velociraptor was also a scavenger. This means it ate meat left by other animals. The velociraptor also ate eggs.

Glossary

carnivore animal that eats meat

fossil bones or other remains of a long dead animal or plant

prey animal that is hunted by another animal

scavenger animal that eats meat left behind by other animals

scientist person who studies the way the world works

species group of animals with similar features

Read more

Dinosaur A to Z: An Amazing Alphabetical Dinosaur Parade, DK (DK Children, 2017)

A Weekend with Dinosaurs (Fantasy Field Trips), Claire Throp (Raintree, 2015)

World's Smallest Dinosaurs (Extreme Dinosaurs), Rupert Matthews (Raintree, 2012)

Websites

www.bbc.co.uk/cbeebies/curations/dinosaur-facts

www.dkfindout.com/uk/dinosaurs-and-prehistoric-life/dinosaurs/velociraptor

Comprehension questions

1. Why do you think velociraptors could not fly?
2. How do scientists know that velociraptors lived in Asia?
3. How do they know that velociraptors ate other dinosaur species?

Index